Easy Concertos and Concertinos

for Violin and Piano

O. Rieding

Concerto

in G

Op.34

(1st position)

Bosworth

Concert in G dur.

Concerto in G major.

O. Rieding, Op. 34.

B.& C⁰ 13261

Bosworth & C⁰

Concert in G dur.

Concerto in G major.

pour Violon

Concert in G dur.

Concerto in G major.

Violine.

O. Rieding, Op. 34.

B. & Cº 13261

Violine.

Violine.

Allegro.

B & Cº 13261